A SAVIOR TO SERVE

Study by Michael Ruffin
Commentary by Judson Edwards

Free downloadable Teaching Guide for this study available at
NextSunday.com/teachingguides

NextSunday Resources
6316 Peake Road
Macon, Georgia 31210-3960
1-800-747-3016
©2019 by NextSunday Resources
All rights reserved.

TABLE OF CONTENTS

A Savior to Serve

HOW TO USE THIS STUDY

NextSunday Resources Adult Bible Studies are designed to help adults study Scripture seriously within the context of the larger Christian tradition and, through that process, find their faith renewed, challenged, and strengthened. We study the Scriptures because we believe they affect our current lives in important ways. Each study contains the following three components:

Study Guide

Each study guide lesson is arranged in four movements:

Reflecting recalls a contemporary story, anecdote, example, or illustration to help us anticipate the session's relevance in our lives.

Studying is centered on giving the biblical material in-depth attention while often surrounding it with helpful insights from theology, ethics, church history, and other areas.

Understanding helps us find relevant connections between our lives and the biblical message.

What About Me? provides brief statements that help unite life issues with the meaning of the biblical text.

Commentary

Each study guide lesson is accompanied by an additional, in-depth commentary on the biblical material. Written by a different author than the study guide, each commentary gives the opportunity for learners to approach the Scripture text from a separate but complementary viewpoint.

Teaching Guide

In addition to the provided study guide and commentary, *NextSunday Resources* also provides a *free* downloadable teaching guide, available at NextSunday.com. Each teaching guide gives the teacher tools for focusing on the content of each study guide lesson through additional commentary and Bible background information. Through teacher helps and teaching options, each teaching guide also provides substance for variety and choice in the preparation of each lesson.

NextSunday
Resources

STUDY INTRODUCTION

We have a Savior to serve. That is our theme during the season of Lent. Really, though, that is our theme all the time. We are called to follow and to serve our Savior in the same ways that he followed and served his Father. We will find that if our lives are based on following Jesus, we will serve him and we will serve our fellow travelers along life's road. We will also find that it is a very costly and very rewarding way to live.

While serving Jesus should be our theme all the time, it is good to have special times during which we can focus on our discipleship. Lent and Holy Week offer special opportunities to do just that. Hopefully, our focus on this theme during this season will inspire us to reflect on it as we live our lives from now on.

The lessons in this unit are all based primarily on Mark's account of Holy Week, those days leading up to Jesus' crucifixion on Good Friday. So the words Jesus spoke and the actions he carried out in our Gospel texts were spoken and done during a time of great tension, controversy, and danger that called for his great commitment, dedication, faith, and determination.

This final week was also a time full of opportunities for Jesus' disciples to learn how to live in times of tension, controversy, and danger, which they would have to do soon enough. They learned their lessons the hard way, through much misunderstanding and failure. We most likely will learn our lessons the same way. Perhaps our study of these texts will give us an opportunity, in the safety of our church and class, to make progress in our commitment to serve our Savior faithfully under the dangerous and trying circumstances that can confront those who follow the way of Christ.

We need the Lord's help to make that kind of progress. We also need each other's help.

It was a hard journey for Jesus and his disciples. Let's go with them and see where the road leads us.

1

A COMMANDMENT
TO KEEP

Deuteronomy 6:4-9; Mark 12:28-34

Central Question

What does it mean to love God fully?

Scripture

Deuteronomy 6:4-9 Israel, listen! Our God is the LORD! Only the LORD! 5 Love the LORD your God with all your heart, all your being, and all your strength. 6 These words that I am command-ing you today must always be on your minds. 7 Recite them to your children. Talk about them when you are sitting around your house and when you are out and about, when you are lying down and when you are getting up. 8 Tie them on your hand as a sign. They should be on your forehead as a symbol. 9 Write them on your house's doorframes and on your city's gates.

Mark 12:28-34 One of the legal experts heard their dispute and saw how well Jesus answered them. He came over and asked him, "Which commandment is the most important of all?" 29 Jesus replied, "The most important one is *Israel, listen! Our God is the one Lord,* 30 *and you must love the Lord your God with all your heart, with all your being, with all your mind, and with all your strength.* 31 The second is this, *You will love your neighbor as yourself.* No other commandment is greater than these." 32 The legal expert said to him, "Well said, Teacher. You have truthfully said that God is one and there is no other besides him. 33 And to love God with all of the heart, a full understanding, and all of one's strength, and to love one's neighbor as oneself is much more important than all kinds of entirely burned offerings and sacrifices." 34 When Jesus saw that he had answered with wisdom, he said to him, "You aren't far from God's kingdom." After that, no one dared to ask him any more questions.

Reflecting

My father loved to tell the story about a young man who was courting a young lady during that long-ago time when folks wrote letters. As my father told it, the love-struck fellow penned such a letter to the object of his fancy.

"Darling," he wrote, "I love you more than anything. For you I would climb the highest mountain. I would swim the deepest river. I would cross the widest desert. And I'll see you on Saturday night—if it's not raining."

The young lady might have had doubts about the reality of her suitor's love, although she would have no cause to question his skills at hyperbole!

Biblically speaking, love comes down to commitment and loyalty. For God to love us is for God to be committed to faithfulness in relationship with us. Likewise, for us to love God is for us to be committed in our relationship with God.

God's commitment to us is total. We see it in how God has acted toward us in many ways but especially in how God has acted toward us in Jesus Christ. We are constantly growing into total commitment to God. We show it in many ways but especially in how we act toward other people.

How do we develop such a love for God? How do we demonstrate it?

> Are we more likely to approach Jesus seeking to listen to him or to find a reason not to listen to him?

Studying

The context of this lesson's passage from Mark is the last week of Jesus' life. Previous events of the week have brought two issues to the forefront. The first issue is the increasing irrelevance and coming destruction of the temple, brought to the fore by Jesus' cleansing of the temple on Monday (11:15-19). Second, the issue of Jesus' authority comes to the fore because of a challenge to his authority by various leaders (11:27-33). This challenge took place earlier on Tuesday, the same day that the events of our passage occur.

Given these events, it is no surprise to find Jesus later on Tuesday embroiled in controversy. Group after group—priests, elders, legal experts, supporters of Herod, Pharisees, and Sadducees—have approached Jesus with questions they hoped would trip him up or force him to give answers that would get him into trouble.

Jesus had handled all of their challenges successfully when along comes a legal expert who, apparently impressed with the answers Jesus had given, wanted to ask him another question. This question, though, appears designed not to entrap Jesus but rather to engage him in a serious and important discussion.

> Legal experts or "scribes" were trained to interpret Jewish law. In the Gospel of Mark, they are usually cast as Jesus' opponents (see, for example, Mark 1:22; 2:6, 16; 3:22; 7:1-5; 8:31; 9:14; 10:33; 11:18; 12:38-40; 14:1, 43, 53; 15:1, 31).

The man's question is, "Which commandment is the most important of all?" (v. 28). This was another way of asking, "Which commandment best summarizes all of the requirements of the law?" Given the large number of commandments contained in the Bible, we can understand the scribe's desire to arrive at such a summary statement.

Jesus' reply combines two Old Testament passages: Deuteronomy 6:4-5 and Leviticus 19:18. So far as anyone can determine, Jesus was the first person to combine those two passages. That is not to say, however, that Jesus originated the idea of joining love for God with love for neighbor. Indeed, the organization of the Ten Commandments itself combines these two concerns with the "first table" having to do with expressing love for God and the "second table" dealing with expressing love for other people. Moreover, the Hebrew prophets consistently insisted that genuine devotion to God and just treatment of people go together (see Mic 6:6-8; Jer 7:1-11, etc.).

The passage from Deuteronomy is known as the Shema after the first word in the Hebrew text, "listen." The Shema was perhaps the most important confession in Judaism. Depending on translation, it affirms either the oneness of God or the unique role God played in Israel's life—or both.

Jesus' quotation of the Shema makes the point that they were and are to love God with their total being—heart, soul, mind, and strength. Deuteronomy 6:6-9 tells the Hebrews to treasure these words and instructs the people to engage in practices that, if followed, would ensure that the teachings of God would become part of the fabric of their lives.

One set of practices involved talking. The people were to teach their children the commandments of the Lord and talk about these commandments at all times (vv. 6-7).

Another set of practices involved symbol-making. The people were to attach the commandments to their hands, foreheads, doorposts, and gates (vv. 7-9). It is possible that the language here was intended as metaphorical. They might mean something like, "Keep the commandments so close to you that it is as if they are attached to your body and your house." In practice, however, Jews came to observe these commandments literally as well. People attached phylacteries, small boxes containing portions of the law, to their arms and forehead, and a box called a mezuzah to their doorposts.

> What practices can we adopt to make Scripture part of the fabric of our lives?

While any practice can be reduced to empty legalism, the intent was to help the people develop and demonstrate their all-encompassing love for God. That is the purpose of our spiritual practices as well.

Jesus adds a second commandment to the first with the implication that they are to be treated as "1a" and "1b." The second commandment, "You will love your neighbor as yourself" (Mark 12:31), comes from Leviticus 19:18. This commandment emphasizes the necessity of sound ethics in dealing with our fellow human beings.

Not surprisingly, the legal expert demonstrates in his response to Jesus great familiarity with Scripture. Perhaps surprisingly, given the assumptions we generally make about Jewish leaders in the Gospels, he agrees with Jesus. In his agreement, he demonstrates that his command of Scripture extends beyond legalism to insight into the spirit of the Scriptures.

The legal expert summarizes and agrees with Jesus' assessment of the heart of the Torah (vv. 32-33). He then alludes to 1 Samuel 15:22 (Card, 152) in his comment, "To love God with all of the heart...and to love one's neighbor as oneself is much more important than all kinds of entirely burned offerings and sacrifices" (v. 33). He affirms that loving attitudes and actions are more important than the correct performance of religious rituals.

The legal expert was impressed with Jesus' answer, and Jesus was impressed with the legal expert's response. Jesus told him, "You aren't far from God's kingdom" (v. 34).

Perhaps we can move toward understanding what Jesus meant by comparing this story to the story in Mark that is most similar to it: the story of the rich man who asked Jesus what he had to do to inherit eternal life (Mark 10:17-22). When Jesus responds with a summary of the commandments having to do with the right treatment of the neighbor, the man says that he has kept those since his youth. Jesus then tells him that he will have treasure in heaven if he sells his possessions, gives the money to the poor, and follows Jesus. The man then goes away grieving, apparently unable to do what Jesus told him.

Jesus knew that despite his understanding and even keeping of the law, the rich man was far from the kingdom because he was not prepared to give himself over completely to God. Perhaps Jesus told the legal expert that he was not far from the kingdom because Jesus perceived that in his heart he was almost ready to give himself over completely to God—no matter what it took.

Understanding

Life is complicated. We can find ourselves being pulled in many directions simultaneously. In living such a complex and demanding life, we need a center from which to operate. As Christians, we know that the center upon which we organize our lives is our relationship with God.

But "our relationship with God" is a broad reality. We need a way to focus on what matters most in that relationship. We turn to the Bible for guidance, but the Bible is a big and deep book. We need a way to organize how we understand its teachings and put them into practice. This was the kind of focus the legal expert sought. Like us, he needed and wanted a way to approach life that would give him confidence that he was living the life that God expected him to live.

While Jesus did not spell out how to go about loving God with one's entire being and loving one's neighbor as oneself, we can learn a lot by paying attention to the context of the Old Testament passages that Jesus quoted.

The commandment to love God comes from a larger passage that encourages specific spiritual practices. It follows, therefore, that we show our love for God by taking whatever steps we can to weave God's teachings into the fabric of our lives.

The commandment to love one's neighbor comes from a larger passage that encourages just treatment of one's fellows. It follows that we show our love for our neighbors by treating them fairly and justly.

What About Me?

• *Will I commit to being fully committed to God?* Sometimes we say that we want to "put God first," but perhaps it would be better to say that we want to "put God only." If you work toward constantly giving your full devotion to God, then everything else will not be given its proper place. Rather, everything will become part of your devotion to God.

• *Will I pursue practices that will put me in a position to grow in my love for God?* Through the centuries, Christians have adopted many means to the end of opening their lives up to the presence and love of God. These means include prayer, Scripture reading, worship, meditations, and service to others. Such practices can help our love for God—our total commitment to God—to become stronger and deeper as we live our lives.

• *Will I live out my love for God through loving actions toward others?* Love, as the Bible means it, is faithful commitment that reveals itself in actions: "God so loved the world that he gave his only Son" (John 3:16). We show our love for others by giving ourselves up for them. But how do we do that? How can we go about giving up our time, our treasure, our pride, and whatever else we have to sacrifice for the sake of others?

Resources

Michael Card, Mark: *The Gospel of Passion* (Downers Grove IL: InterVarsity, 2012).

T. J. Mashburn III, "Scribe in the New Testament," *Mercer Dictionary of the Bible* (Macon GA: Mercer University Press, 1990).

A COMMANDMENT TO KEEP

Deuteronomy 6:4-9; Mark 12:28-34

Introduction

In case you haven't noticed, life has gotten complicated. I was reminded of that recently when I received a brochure from my cable company informing me of all the television channels I can now watch. Though I'm dating myself when I write this, I can remember a time when I had three choices: ABC, NBC, and CBS. But I now have access to several hundred stations. There are over forty *sports* channels available to me. Needless to say, I will never watch most of the channels on my television.

That same phenomenon is true when it comes to the magazines I will read, the phone I will use, the groceries I will buy, and even the church I will attend. Once I had a few simple options; now I'm drowning in choices. I'm not saying I want to go back to that simpler world. I kind of like having twelve different brands of peanut butter to choose from in the grocery store. But having all these choices has complicated my life.

That same confusing number of alternatives confronts us when it comes to God. Who knows what to believe any more? There are so many religions, denominations, even so many flavors of Baptists or Presbyterians, that it is easy to get bewildered by it all. Many of us can identify with those people who said to Jesus, "If you are the Christ, tell us plainly" (John 10:24). Like our New Testament counterparts, we long for someone to cut through the confusion and tell us plainly what to believe.

What is Christianity about anyway? What's the essence of it all? In a world of so many spiritual options, how can we know what to believe? Maybe more importantly, how can we know *whom* to believe?

Because those questions are so crucial to our lives, we are forever indebted to that unnamed religious leader who came to Jesus with the question, "Which commandment is the most important of all?" (Mark 12:28). That question gave Jesus the opportunity to sort through all of the laws in the Old Testament and pinpoint the most essential of all. Searching people in every generation have been grateful for that man's question—and Jesus' willingness to answer it.

Cutting through the Confusion

Some biblical interpreters have suggested that this religious leader's motives were less than pure. They suggest that his was a trick question, designed to put Jesus in a no-win situation. By the time of Jesus, the scribes and Pharisees had pinpointed 613 Old Testament laws the devout were supposed to keep. How could Jesus possibly pick just one of those 613 as the most important?

Certainly, the scribes and Pharisees were not above trying to trick Jesus and make him look foolish, but let's give this teacher the benefit of the doubt. Let's assume the best about him and let him be one of us.

What if he, like us, was drowning in options? What if he, like us, was bewildered by all of the religion he had to digest? What if he was truly asking Jesus to cut through the fluff and get to what is essential? That teacher might well have been saying to Jesus, "We teachers of the law have identified 613 laws we're supposed to be keeping, 613 things we're supposed to do and believe. Tell us the most important of all. I'm getting tired of sorting through all of these 'oughts' and 'shoulds.' It seems to me we're drowning in minutiae. Can you tell us the number one thing we need to know?"

There comes a time in your theological education when the important thing is not learning more truth but prioritizing the truth you already know. Some of us have been in church all of our lives. We know a lot about the Bible, theology, and church history. We've heard a thousand and one sermons on the prodigal son. We're at the point in our lives where we don't need more information. Rather, we need to prioritize the information we already have. What, among this pile of truths we've accumulated, is paramount?

It would have been understandable if Jesus had chosen not to answer that religious leader's question. Who could possibly pick the one most important commandment out of 613 possibilities? Why fall into the Pharisees' trap if you didn't have to? Why not give some nebulous, evasive answer and move on down the road?

But, to his everlasting credit, Jesus didn't do that. He looked that man right in the eye and gave him a straightforward reply: "The most important one is *Israel, listen! Our God is the one Lord, and you must love the Lord your God with all your heart, with all your being, with all your mind, and with all your strength*. The second is this, *You will love your neighbor as yourself*. No other commandment is greater than these" (Mark 12:29-31).

Out of all of those commandments in the law, Jesus picked Deuteronomy 6:4-5 and Leviticus 19:8. He grafted those two commandments together to come up with the single most important commandment of all. Condense all of those prophetic harangues in the Old Testament, all of those impossible laws in Leviticus, all of those strange biblical stories that seem so foreign to our modern experience, and here's what they're trying to teach us: love God and love people.

Our charter, when all the doctrinal clutter is swept away, is to love God with our whole being and to love others as much as we love ourselves. That is what it means to keep the commandments.

Loving God

The first part of the great commandment is that we love God with all of our heart, being, mind, and strength. Jesus added that phrase "with all your mind" to the original verse from Deuteronomy. The point is that we are to love God with every fiber of our being, with all of the components at our disposal. Our lives are supposed to be God-soaked, God-saturated, and God-focused.

But, of course, everybody knows that. Let the preacher announce from the pulpit this Sunday that we should all love God, and we will nod in agreement but be unmoved by his words. A preacher announcing that people are to love God is like a botanist calling a news conference to announce that grass is green. It's true, but we've known that all of our lives. Tell us something new.

But as old hat as this proclamation is, it is still the great commandment. We are to love God with our heart, being, mind, and strength. If we don't love God, we're living half a life, and we don't have a clue what the Bible is about.

We are to love God, be sensitive to God, worship God, pray to God, dance with the mystery of God, be honest with God, sing to God, read about God, talk to one another about God, teach our children about God, and be grateful to God for all of our blessings.

And sometimes we forget that. We get caught up in "stuff" and forget God. One of our old hymns says it well: "Prone to wander, Lord, I feel it. Prone to leave the God I love." We're all prone to leave the God we love, which is why it's important to read Mark 12:34-40 on a regular basis just to remember our marching orders.

Loving People

The second part of the great commandment is that we love our neighbor as we love ourselves. In Jesus' mind, it was impossible to love God without loving people. Those two things are inseparable, like breathing in and out. We prove our love for God by loving others. So, Jesus added a line from Leviticus 19 to the line from Deuteronomy 6 and together they give us the great commandment.

The reason this second part of the great commandment is crucial is because we humans can't live without love. Perhaps we should tie a wristband on every baby when they're born that says, "This person must be touched, loved, listened to, and delighted in, or she will die." Then we should make it mandatory that every person wear that wristband all through life.

That way, when we take our baby home from the hospital, we can look at that wristband and remember that message through those sleepless nights and colic and the "terrible two's." When she becomes a surly teenager, testing the limits, trying to discover who she is in a scary world, we can look at the wristband...and love her. When she goes off to college, gets married, gets to be middle-aged and somewhat disillusioned with her life, we can remember the indispensability of loving her. And when she goes off to the nursing home, old and tired and lonely, someone can look at her wristband and remember that she will die unless someone loves her.

Everyone we know deserves one of those wristbands. Without love, people become sad, sick, and desperate. Without love, they can't function. Love is the fuel that helps people move through life with joy and purpose, and, when they have it, they are amazingly resilient. But when they don't have love in their lives, bad things happen—physically, emotionally, relationally, and spiritually.

In his book *Love in Four Dimensions* (Nashville TN: Broadman, 1982), William Hull writes, "While we need not minimize the threat of atomic annihilation, its destruction for many would be mercifully swift, whereas death from not being loved is always slow and painful. No bomb has been invented that can inflict as much cruelty on the vital part of our being as the blight of feeling that no one cares" (70). No wonder Jesus added the line about loving our neighbors to the great commandment. He of all people knew about the indispensability of love. More than anyone in human history, he saw that invisible wristband on the people around him and loved them with all of his heart.

Conclusion

When Jesus finished spelling out the great commandment, the legal expert agreed with him. Unlike many of the religious leaders of the day, he thought Jesus was on the right track: "To love God with all of the heart, a full understanding, and all of one's strength, and to love one's neighbor as oneself is much more important than all kinds of entirely burned offerings and sacrifices" (v. 33).

When Jesus heard that, he said to the man, "You aren't far from God's kingdom" (v. 34). This man was definitely moving in the right direction. He was starting to get it. A life with God, he realized, involved the two priorities Jesus had identified: loving God with one's whole being and loving one's neighbor as oneself.

Burnt offerings and sacrifices couldn't hold a candle to loving God and people.

But notice that Jesus didn't say that the man had arrived. He wasn't far from God's kingdom, but he wasn't there yet. Why? What was he still lacking? He seems to be so far ahead of most of his contemporaries that you might think Jesus would say he had arrived in the kingdom. But something was still missing.

I think what was missing was action. This legal expert knew the great commandment with his mind. He knew what Jesus said was true. But only when he started putting the great commandment into action would he fully step into the kingdom.

If he went home from his encounter with Jesus determined to pray, worship, and take delight in God as never before; if he threw his arms around his wife and whirled her around the room; if he took his son by the hand and took him fishing at the local pond; if he went to see his aged mother, bringing her favorite soup; if he started respecting and conversing with his fellow legal experts (even those with a different theology), then and only then would he enter the kingdom of God. He had taken the first step by understanding the essence of a life with God, but he still had another gigantic step to take.

You see, it's one thing to *know* the great commandment; it's another thing altogether to *live* it.

Notes

Notes

2

A WARNING
TO HEED

Daniel 11:21. 30-35; Mark 13:5-13

Central Question

How can I respond to evil in my world?

Scripture

Daniel 11:21, 30-35 A worthless person will arise in his place. Royal majesty will not have been given to him, but he will come in a time of security and seize the kingdom by deceitful means.... 30 Kittim ships will fight against him, and he will retreat in fear. He will rage against a holy covenant and will do what he wants. Then he will pay special attention to those who violate a holy covenant. 31 His forces will come and make the sanctuary fortress impure. They will stop the daily sacrifice and set up a desolating monstrosity. 32 By deceitful means he will corrupt those who violate a covenant, but the people who acknowledge their God will stand strong and will act. 33 "The people's teachers will help many understand, but for a time they will fall by sword and by flame, by captivity and by plunder. 34 When they fall, they will receive a little help, but many will join them with deceitful plans. 35 Some of the teachers too will fall in order that they might be refined, purified, and cleansed—until an end time, because it is still not yet the set time."

Mark 13:5-13 Jesus said, "Watch out that no one deceives you. 6 Many people will come in my name, saying, 'I'm the one!' They will deceive many people. 7 When you hear of wars and reports of wars, don't be alarmed. These things must happen, but this isn't the end yet. 8 Nations and kingdoms will fight against each other, and there will be earthquakes and famines in all sorts of places. These things are just the beginning of the sufferings associated with the end. 9 "Watch out for yourselves. People will hand you over to the councils. You will be beaten in the synagogues. You will stand before governors and kings because of me so that you can testify before them. 10 First, the good news must be proclaimed to all the nations. 11 When they haul you in and hand you over, don't worry ahead of time about what to answer or say. Instead, say whatever is given to you at that moment, for you aren't doing the speaking but the Holy Spirit is. 12 Brothers and sisters will hand each other over to death. A father will turn in his children. Children will rise up against their parents and have them executed. 13 Everyone will hate you because of my name. But whoever stands firm until the end will be saved."

Reflecting

In the fall of 2013, we were in the first days of a United States government shutdown and in the throes of a crisis in Syria. As you are discussing this lesson, hopefully similar crises are not confronting us, but chances are very good that they are. There are always crises, aren't there? Such is the way of the world.

Followers of Jesus need to grow in our ability to discern between the signs of the times that are the signs of all times and the signs that may be particular to our time. Our greater need, however—indeed, our calling from Jesus—is to react appropriately to what we see and experience.

We do not want to overreact to what happens around us and to us. After all, evil and disaster are present in every period of history. Jesus summons us, as he summoned all believers in every generation, to be faithful in our proclamation of his good news with both our actions and our words, no matter the evil we may encounter.

At the same time, we don't want to underreact to what happens around us and to us. After all, evil and disaster are real. We shouldn't treat them as if they

What crises, large or small, have captured your attention in recent days? How are you responding to them?

aren't significant. Jesus calls us to counter faithlessness with faithfulness, despair with trust, and danger with hope. When it looks like the end of the world is near, we are to live as those who believe in the future that God has in store.

The fact is that we face evil in every moment of every era. The question is not whether but rather how we will respond.

Studying

It is Tuesday, three days before Good Friday. Jesus and his disciples are in Jerusalem for the Passover festival. Like all Passover pilgrims, they have visited the massive temple complex. As they leave the temple, one of the disciples remarks about the size of the stones used to construct it (Mark 13:1). Archaeologists have uncovered stones used in the construction of the temple platform that weigh over 300 tons. The largest discovered weighed around 415 tons and measured 46 feet long, 10 feet high, and 10 feet wide (Drinkard, 880). The temple that was rebuilt by Herod the Great beginning around 20 BC was one of the most remarkable structures in the ancient world.

It is not difficult, therefore, to imagine the shock that disciple experienced when Jesus responded to his question by saying, "Do you see these enormous buildings? Not even one stone will be left upon another. All will be demolished" (v. 2).

Later, while sitting on the Mount of Olives, some of Jesus' disciples asked him about what he had said: "Tell us, when will these things happen? What sign will show that all these things are about to come to an end?" (v. 4). It is possible that the first "these things" refers to the pending destruction of the temple while "all these things" refers to the events that would accompany the approaching end. Regardless, Jesus' response, the beginning

of which is in this lesson's Gospel passage, sounds a cautionary note. The disciples must be aware of what is coming so that they will be prepared to persevere in carrying out their ministry. They are not, however, to become obsessed with unfolding events and thus be dissuaded from completing this task.

Jesus does not answer the disciples' question directly. Instead, he issues warnings. The first warning is that they not follow false leaders who claim to be the Messiah (vv. 5-6). History has shown and experience continues to show that crises provide an opportunity for demagogues, charlatans, and egomaniacs who prey on people's fears. In our day and time, to follow such a leader would probably cost us only money, time, and embarrassment. In the first century, though, with the power of Rome to contend with, such a movement usually led to the death of the leader and often to the deaths of his followers. Such a false leader could even go to the extreme of declaring himself to be the returned Messiah, claiming the authority ("in my name") and even the identity ("I'm the one") of Jesus (v. 6). Jesus' disciples are not to follow such people.

Jesus goes on to say that his disciples shouldn't let political or natural upheavals lead them to believe that the end is near. Our Daniel passage deals with a crisis brought about in Judah when the Seleucid ruler Antiochus IV Epiphanes assumed power in the second century BC. In Jesus' day, the Romans were often cast in the role Antiochus played 200 years earlier. Their great military and political power threatened to wipe the Jews from the face of the earth. As we read this lesson's passage, it reminds us that tensions and threats—and even persecution—can and do come to God's people in every age.

> Daniel 11:21-45 refers to the rule of Antiochus IV Epiphanes (175–164 BC). This Greek Syrian king was determined to make Greek culture the standard way of life in Judea, which put him at odds with pious Jews. He was eventually defeated in a rebellion led by the family known as the Maccabees. Details of the story can be found in the books of 1–2 Maccabees in the Apocrypha.

Due to political maneuvering in Rome and unrest in Palestine, the first century was rife with "wars and reports of wars" (v. 7). In particular, Mark's Gospel may have been written

during the time of the Jewish Revolt of AD 66–70. This conflict resulted in the destruction of Jerusalem and its temple. But even this war couldn't be seen as a necessary sign of the end. Jesus' followers are not to be alarmed because "these things must happen" (v. 7). That is, such things are not only the way of the world, they also somehow fit into the plans and purposes of God (v. 7). Disciples of Jesus are to live faithfully through such events as they occur. They mustn't take them as signs that the end is imminent, for "this isn't the end yet" (v. 7). They are to look for ways to live in the dangerous world rather than for a way to get out of it.

In addition, Jesus' followers were not to be misled by earthquakes and famines (v. 8). Such events, cataclysmic though they might seem, were merely the initial stages of the labor into which creation was entering and which it still endures (see Rom 8:18-23). Birth pangs are to be lived through for the sake of the blessing that comes at the end. They are not to be avoided.

Jesus warned his disciples of the persecution they would undergo because of the ordinary upheavals of the world and also because they were followers of Christ. For proclaimers of the good news, such persecution is to be expected. These things would happen "because of me" (v. 9) and "because of my name" (v. 13). For someone to "hand you over" (v. 11) is what happens to those who are identified with and who preach Jesus. It happened to Jesus himself (Mark 10:33), and it will happen to his followers (Culpepper, 453).

Words of warning alternate with words of commission in verses 9-13. Jesus warns his disciples that both Jewish and Roman

Each detail of Jesus' words found its fulfillment in the four decades leading up to the destruction of the temple in AD 70. Five major earthquakes occurred: in Crete (AD 46), Rome (AD 51), Phrygia (AD 53, 60), and Campania (AD 63). There were three great famines during the reign of Claudius: in Judea (AD 44), Greece (AD 50) and Rome (AD 52). In addition, AD 65 was the worst year for famines and earthquakes in the entire history of Rome, and AD 69, known as the "year of the four emperors," was a time of political confusion and upheaval the likes of which Rome had never experienced. (Card, 159).

authorities will persecute them, but they are still to preach the good news to all nations (vv. 9-10). They will be brought to trial, but they are to depend on the Holy Spirit to give them the words to say (v. 11). They will be betrayed and hated, but they are to endure to the end (vv. 12-13). They must look upon their times of trial as opportunities to share the good news of the kingdom. Jesus' followers are to be faithful in such proclamation.

Jesus does not promise to rescue his followers from persecution. He promises them rather that they will have what they need to continue to minister in the midst of persecution and that they will experience rescue ("will be saved," v. 13) once they have endured to the end.

Understanding

We Christians who live in countries in which we enjoy religious freedom should be duly hesitant to assert that the slights and barbs that we might occasionally endure qualify as persecution. This would be an insult to our sisters and brothers who live in places where their faith puts them at genuine risk.

Unlike many Christians around the world, we are not hauled before councils and courts, and our family members are not turning us over to be executed. Although we might sometimes be misunderstood and ridiculed, we don't face the kind of danger the early followers of Jesus faced and that believers in many parts of the world face today. When it comes to persecution, most of us would be better off praying for and trying to help those who are really experiencing it.

At the same time, though, no matter where we live, we all face a dangerous world. National and international conflicts, be they social, political, or military, remind us of our vulnerability. Natural disasters can strike anyone anywhere with devastating force and exact a tremendous cost. While not likely, organized persecution is not unimaginable. Evil seems more present than ever. If it is not more prevalent in reality, it is more pervasive in its presentation through the media now available to us and forced upon us. The temptation to give in to frustration and despair is real, and so is the temptation to do nothing.

Jesus warns us against such inaction. He spurs us on to committed and faithful action in the face of any and all threats. He wants us to understand that the world is the way it is and that we are to bring his good news to bear in a world where evil is rampant. Proclamation and perseverance are to be our watchwords.

What About Me?

• *Am I aware of how evil reveals itself in my surroundings?* It is easy to think that we understand how evil rears its head on the national and international scene. Sometimes it is harder to see it when it is close to home. Also, some of its more local manifestations may be more subtle than obvious.

• *Is it possible that we sometimes call evil good?* Do we avoid the risk of persecution for our faith because we don't, in fact, follow Jesus in the narrow way that runs counter to some of the predominant ways of our culture? Do we stop to think about how some of the accepted ways of living in our setting are not true to the way of Jesus?

• *Do I allow the reality of evil to inspire me to action or do I let it depress me into inaction?* The way things are is the context in which we are called to be who we are and to do what we do, but we are called to bear witness to the way things could be.

• *Am I committed to persevering to the end?* Am I taking steps to strengthen my faith so that I will endure? Jesus persevered to the end; he persevered all the way to the cross. Are we committed to enduring no matter what the cost?

Resources

Michael Card, *Mark: The Gospel of Passion* (Downers Grove IL: InterVarsity, 2012).

R. Alan Culpepper, *Mark*, Smyth & Helwys Bible Commentary (Macon GA: Smyth & Helwys, 2007).

Joel F. Drinkard Jr., "Temple/Temples," *Mercer Dictionary of the Bible*, ed. Watson E. Mills et al. (Macon GA: Mercer University Press, 1990).

A WARNING
TO HEED

Daniel 11:21, 30-35; Mark 13:5-13

Introduction

In *The New Daily Study Bible on the Gospel of Mark* (Louisville KY: Westminster John Knox, 2001), William Barclay writes,

> Mark 13 is one of the most difficult chapters in the New Testament for a modern reader to understand. That is because it is one of the most Jewish chapters in the Bible. From beginning to end it is thinking in terms of Jewish history and Jewish ideas. All through it Jesus is using categories and pictures which were familiar to the Jews of his day, but which are very strange, and, indeed, unknown, to many modern readers. Even so, it is not possible to disregard this chapter because it is the source of many ideas about the second coming of Jesus. (353)

We're focusing this lesson on nine verses from this difficult chapter, verses in which Jesus gives a somber warning to his followers about coming catastrophes. Just as the prophet Daniel did in Daniel 11, Jesus looks into the future and sees wars, troubles, and suffering. But he also sees what Daniel saw: "The people who acknowledge their God will stand strong and will act" (Dan 11:32).

Jesus' warning in Mark 13:5-13 is a mixture of both horror and hope. There are some ominous warnings about the future, for sure, but some hopeful promises about the future as well.

Ominous Warnings about the Future

When the curtain rises on Mark 13, one of the disciples of Jesus is commenting on the impressive splendor of the temple in

Jerusalem. Jesus responds by saying that the awesome, enormous building will one day be reduced to rubble. Then Peter, James, John, and Andrew ask him privately, "Tell us, when will these things happen? What sign will show that all these things are about to come to an end?" (v. 4).

That question gives Jesus an opportunity to talk about several things. One reason Mark 13 is confusing is because Jesus seems to refer to several different things in the same chapter, and we're not always sure what he is referencing. In Mark 13, Jesus refers to (1) the destruction of Jerusalem (vv. 1-2, 14-20), (2) the coming persecution of believers (vv. 9-13), (3) the dangers of the last days (vv. 3-6, 21-22), (4) his second coming (vv. 7-8, 24-27), and (5) the necessity of believers to be on watch (vv. 28-37).

The verses we're studying touch on three of these issues:

• *The dangers of the last days* (vv. 5-6). Deceptive people will claim to be following Jesus, when, in fact, they are not followers at all.
• *Christ's second coming* (vv. 7-8). Before the end comes, there will be wars and reports of wars, earthquakes and famines, and other "sufferings associated with the end" (v. 8).
• *The coming persecution of believers* (vv. 9-13). Jesus' followers will be brought before government authorities, beaten in synagogues, and hated by their own families.

This picture of the end times doesn't exactly fill us with hope, does it? And we comfortable Americans have a hard time identifying with what Jesus says in these verses. It's hard for us to fathom that much deception, suffering, and persecution. If the end times are going to bring such misery, most of us find ourselves praying, "Lord, take me now!"

But we should remember that many people in history would have read these verses and identified completely with what Jesus said. Ironically, as I was typing this paragraph, I decided to take a break and go onto the home page on my computer. The lead story on the home page said, "After giving her three days to recant her faith, a judge in Sudan has sentenced a pregnant 27-year-old woman to death for being a Christian." It's hard for us comfortable Americans to imagine that kind of world, but that woman in Sudan would have no trouble at all relating to Mark 13. This woman is living it.

Many suffering Christians in our world would read Mark 13 and think we must be in the end times now because they have experienced all of the things Jesus describes. They have dealt with more than their share of deceptive people. They have experienced wars and natural disasters. And they have been persecuted because of their faith in Jesus. Unlike us, they would read Mark 13 and identify with it completely.

Certainly, Jesus' first followers would have understood the significance of his words. Following Jesus would not be easy. The future would be filled with peril. Their commitment to Christ would not protect them from trouble. On the contrary, it would put them squarely in the middle of it.

Hopeful Promises about the Future

When we read these sayings of Jesus about the future, we understand the significance of his words, too. This is not a feel-good passage. It is a wake-up call that tells us that being a Christian is not always easy or popular. In fact, reading Jesus' predictions about the future can be downright depressing!

But there is a glimmer of hope amidst these ominous predictions. In verses 10-11 and 13, Jesus gave his followers some advice about how to deal with all of this coming trouble. If the future did, indeed, hold wars and reports of wars, natural disasters, persecution, and conflict, how could they survive? What should they do in the face of these seemingly insurmountable perils in their future?

Jesus offers them a four-point plan for surviving, and even conquering, the coming trouble. First, he says, *proclaim the good news*. He reminds them that the gospel must be proclaimed to all the nations (v. 10). In the face of their trials and tribulations, they were to remember the good news of Jesus and his death and resurrection. They were to cling to grace and forgiveness. They were to overcome all of the darkness they would have to face with the unquenchable light of the gospel. Not only were they to remember the good news, they were to proclaim it to all the nations.

Second, *don't worry*. When they were handed over to councils, beaten in the synagogues, or brought before Roman leaders, they were not to worry about what they would say. Of course, that's easier said than done. In an old episode of *The Andy Griffith Show*, Andy tells Barney not to be afraid to go into a haunted house by telling him, "There's nothing to fear but fear itself." Barney replies, "But, Andy, that's what I've got: fear itself!" Sometimes we have worry itself, and no matter how hard we try, we drown in worry. Jesus said not to worry, even when we stand eye to eye with the most powerful people in the world.

Third, *trust the Holy Spirit*. The reason the disciples were not to worry was because the Holy Spirit would speak for them. Face to face with those powerful leaders, they would receive surprising help from God's Spirit. The Spirit's work can't be explained. It can only be experienced. But the promise of Scripture is that in our times of greatest need, we will receive unseen help and comfort from an unseen Presence within us. Jesus told his followers to trust the Spirit in their times of trouble and stress.

Fourth, *stand firm until the end*. In verse 13, Jesus says, "But whoever stands firm until the end will be saved." What should his disciples do in a world of wars and reports of wars? Stand firm until the end. What should they do when natural disasters wreak havoc on them and their loved ones? Stand firm until the end. What should they do when they are persecuted for their faith? Stand firm until the end. What should they do when people, even family members, hate them because of their love for Christ? Stand firm until the end. This fourth admonition from Jesus was a way of telling his followers that their endurance would pay off in the end. If they keep on keeping on, they will be saved. On the far side of all of this suffering, there will be victory and celebration.

A Plan for the Future—And for Now

When we study a passage such as Mark 13:5-13, we are reminded that following Jesus is not easy. Even if it seems easy to us, it isn't easy for everyone. Many people have given their lives for the sake of the gospel. Even today, some people in our world still face martyrdom for their beliefs.

One of the best ways to use these verses might be to apply Jesus' counsel to his followers to our own troubles. Mark 13 gives us a picture of the world spinning crazily out of control. Jesus pictures a world of deceptive people, wars, earthquakes and famines, confrontations with powerful people, and families splitting apart. It's a dark, frightening picture.

But frankly, we don't have to wait for the end times to experience those things. I imagine many of us, even now, face situations in which the world seems to be spinning crazily out of control. The darkness is not out there ahead of us, it's happening right now all around us and within us.

Why can't we use Jesus' strategy for dealing with the end times right now in our current out-of-control circumstances? Why can't we face our health issues, family problems, job stresses, and financial strains by doing the four things Jesus commands?

What is most frightening about the darkness is that we often don't have a plan for escaping it. When we feel we're stuck in the darkness forever, we're on the brink of despair. The antidote for surviving any kind of personal darkness is having a plan to get out of that darkness.

When I was a little boy, our family took a trip to Carlsbad Caverns in New Mexico. There was a time in our tour of the caverns when the guide turned off all of the lights to show us how dark it was in that cave. It was so dark we couldn't see anything—not even our own hands in front of our faces. Even as a child, I wasn't afraid. I knew my parents were there beside me. I knew I could hold their hands if I needed to. And I knew that we would soon be in the light again. I didn't despair in that darkness because I had a plan for escaping it.

When we stumble into any kind of darkness in our lives, we need a plan for getting out of it. Jesus' advice in Mark 13 is a good strategy for surviving in the dark. When my life starts spinning out of control, I will hold fast to the good news about Jesus and his love for me. I will try my best not to worry. I will trust the mysterious Holy Spirit working within me and I will hold firm all the way to the end, trusting that if I do endure, I will be saved and walk out into the glorious light.

Conclusion

Before that guide in Carlsbad Caverns turned out all of the lights, he warned us that he was going to do it. He didn't want us to be surprised by the sudden darkness. Even with the warning, though, many people gasped when the lights were turned off.

Jesus didn't want his followers to be surprised by the darkness, either. They needed to know that trouble was coming. But Jesus didn't merely warn them about the darkness. He gave them a plan that would bring them back into the light.

It's a plan that's helpful to remember any time we're plunged into the darkness, either out there at the end of time or, perhaps, today as we struggle to survive in some present crisis.

Blessings on you as you help the members of your class learn to survive in the darkness.

Notes

Notes

A MISSION
TO EMBRACE

Isaiah 61:1-3a; Mark 14:1-9

Central Question

What is the meaning of Christ's anointing?

Scripture

Isaiah 61:1-3a The LORD God's spirit is upon me, because the LORD has anointed me. He has sent me to bring good news to the poor, to bind up the brokenhearted, to proclaim release for captives, and liberation for prisoners, 2 to proclaim the year of the LORD's favor and a day of vindication for our God, to comfort all who mourn, 3 to provide for Zion's mourners, to give them a crown in place of ashes, oil of joy in place of mourning, a mantle of praise in place of discouragement.

Mark 14:1-9 It was two days before Passover and the Festival of Unleavened Bread. The chief priests and legal experts through cunning tricks were searching for a way to arrest Jesus and kill him. 2 But they agreed that it shouldn't happen during the festival; otherwise, there would be an uproar among the people. 3 Jesus was at Bethany visiting the house of Simon, who had a skin disease. During dinner, a woman came in with a vase made of alabaster and containing very expensive perfume of pure nard. She broke open the vase and poured the perfume on his head. 4 Some grew angry. They said to each other, "Why waste the perfume? 5 This perfume could have been sold for almost a year's pay and the money given to the poor." And they scolded her. 6 Jesus said, "Leave her alone. Why do you make trouble for her? She has done a good thing for me. 7 You always have the poor with you; and whenever you want, you can do something good for them. But you won't always have me. 8 She has done what she could. She has anointed my body ahead of time for burial. 9 I tell you the truth that, wherever in the whole world the good news is announced, what she's done will also be told in memory of her."

Reflecting

All of us have probably witnessed the inauguration of an American president. Some of us have watched the coronation of a monarch. Such ceremonies, in which someone assumes a major leadership role, are accompanied by great fanfare and celebration. We would be surprised if, in his or her remarks, a newly inaugurated or crowned leader stood to speak and said, "I am now ready to die."

Yet that is, in effect, what happens in this Gospel lesson. Jesus, who is God's Messiah or "anointed one," is anointed with expensive ointment by an anonymous woman. Jesus interprets that act as preparation for his coming burial. It is through his crucifixion that Jesus will become the king (see Mark 15:26).

The idea of someone becoming a monarch by dying is counterintuitive, but Jesus reveals that this is the way of God. What are the implications of this lesson for how we, subjects of that King, are to live?

Studying

Isaiah 61 was most likely written sometime in the years after the return from the Babylonian exile (538 BC). The words come from a spiritual descendant of the eighth-century prophet Isaiah, whose words became attached to the Isaiah scroll because of the author's affinity with the tradition of that great prophet. This later visionary spoke of one who had received the Lord's anointing.

This anointing involved receiving the Lord's spirit and being commissioned to proclaim the good news of God's salvation.

God intended to set people free from whatever oppressed them (Isa 61:1). The anointed one would "proclaim the year of the LORD's favor" (Isa 61:2), an idealistic vision of the future rooted in the tradition of the Jubilee Year (see Lev 25).

On a Sabbath day early in his ministry, Jesus went to the synagogue in his hometown of Nazareth and read those verses from the book of Isaiah. He then said, "Today, this scripture has been fulfilled just as you heard it" (Luke 4:21). This passage reveals that Jesus saw his life and ministry as the working out of the word the prophet had spoken over five centuries before. Jesus had been anointed by the Spirit of God to set free the oppressed.

Throughout his ministry, Jesus went about setting people free. The prophet's words about the Spirit's anointing were ultimately fulfilled in the life and ministry of Jesus. Jesus' anointing and ministry culminated in the great saving act of his death. In the week before this event, an unnamed woman anointed him, symbolically preparing his body for burial.

That anointing happened on Wednesday of Holy Week, "two days before Passover and the Festival of Unleavened Bread" (Mark 14:1). Passover began with the killing of the Passover lamb on Thursday evening. Most people in the ancient world counted days inclusively, however, so "two days before" in Jewish reckoning actually meant "the day before" (Senior, 43). Passover and the Feast of Unleavened Bread were likely once separate festivals but they had become joined in Jewish practice.

This is not the first time since Jesus entered Jerusalem for the Passover that Mark has noted the desire of the chief priests and

> Jesus went to Nazareth, where he had been raised. On the Sabbath he went to the synagogue as he normally did and stood up to read. The synagogue assistant gave him the scroll from the prophet Isaiah. He unrolled the scroll and found the place where it was written: *The Spirit of the Lord is upon me, because the Lord has anointed me. He has sent me to preach good news to the poor, to proclaim release to the prisoners and recovery of sight to the blind, to liberate the oppressed, and to proclaim the year of the Lord's favor.* He rolled up the scroll, gave it back to the synagogue assistant, and sat down. Every eye in the synagogue was fixed on him. He began to explain to them, "Today, this scripture has been fulfilled just as you heard it." (Luke 4:16-21)

legal experts to arrest and kill him, as well as their hesitation to do so because of the crowds (see 11:18, 32; 12:12). The religious leaders also had used "cunning tricks" (v. 1) throughout the week to try to trap Jesus, especially in the disputes they had with him in the temple the day before (11:27–12:40). Although the conflict is clearly coming to a head, the authorities decide that they can't risk creating turmoil among the people. They no doubt feared the reaction it might bring from the Roman forces that were present in Jerusalem during Passover in greater strength than usual.

Jesus is at Bethany, a town on the Mount of Olives that was his home base during his visit to Jerusalem (11:11-12). He is having dinner in the home of a man named Simon, who is identified only as having "a skin disease" (v. 3). He is otherwise unknown to us. Was Simon a cured leper or did he still bear his disease? Was Jesus having dinner with someone who had once been considered unclean or someone who was still unclean? Regardless, Simon's disease had been or still was serious enough for him to be known by it.

> The "skin disease" is traditionally translated "leprosy," but the underlying Greek word actually covers all manner of skin diseases. It need not refer to Hansen's disease, the modern term for leprosy proper.

Into the dinner came a woman who Mark does not name. There are similar narratives in the other Gospels (Matt 26:6-13; Luke 7:36-50; John 12:1-8), but there are significant differences in setting and characters. In Matthew's story, which is most like Mark's, the woman is also anonymous. In fact, the woman is so anonymous in these accounts that we know absolutely nothing about her other than what she did in breaking open the alabaster vase and pouring its contents on Jesus' head. The vase would have been a "single-use" container. Its narrow neck was broken to allow one to pour out the contents. Therefore, everything in it would have been used. The perfume the woman poured on Jesus' head was made of nard, which was derived from a plant grown in India.

"Some grew angry" (v. 4) at what the woman had done. Although the angry ones are not directly identified in the text,

Jesus' response (vv. 6-9) makes the most sense if it is addressed to his disciples (Culpepper, 485). Their complaints, which they shared with each other before turning their verbal barbs on the woman, were based on the seeming waste and on the obvious extravagance of her act, as the perfume was worth "almost a year's pay" (v. 5). Literally, this was "three hundred denarii," a denarius being the average daily wage for a first-century laborer. The observation that money gained from selling the perfume could have been given to the poor (v. 5) is factually accurate. Moreover, people were expected to give to the poor during Passover.

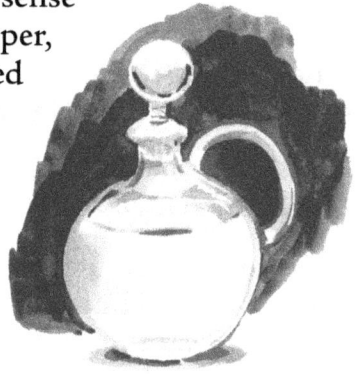

Jesus countered these criticisms by pointing out the positive nature of what the woman had done. In saying, "You always have the poor with you" (v. 7), Jesus was not giving anyone an excuse not to care for the poor. Indeed, Jesus clearly taught that his followers should be concerned about them. When Jesus read from Isaiah 61 in the Nazareth synagogue, he announced that God "has sent me to preach good news to the poor" (Luke 4:18). It is obviously not good news to the poor to have their needs ignored! The contrast isn't between Jesus and the poor, but between "always" and "not always" (Lane, 494).

Still, Jesus judged her act to be a good one (v. 6). Whether or not she realized the full significance of what she did, so far as Jesus was concerned, this woman had anointed his body in preparation for burial (v. 8). She had thus done what would not be done after he was crucified (Mark 15:42–16:1). Such anointing was, of course, usually done after death. For Jesus, then, his death was already as good as accomplished. It was inevitable.

Jesus then said that in the preaching of the good news throughout the

> The issue is not a forced choice between worship and ministry; there is a time for each, and the poor will always be better served by the spontaneous generosity of the unnamed woman than the calculating plans of those who were critical of the beautiful thing she did for Jesus. (Culpepper, 486)

world, the woman's act of service would "be told in memory of her" (v. 9). This lesson is one more fulfillment of Jesus' word. Whoever this woman was, she still serves as a model of heartfelt, sincere, extravagant, loving service.

Understanding

The anointing of Jesus just two days before he was crucified pointed toward his death. Really, though, Jesus' entire life pointed toward his death. God's love and grace as seen in Jesus is self-giving, self-emptying, and self-sacrificing. It could lead nowhere else except to the final giving up of self on the cross.

The woman who anointed Jesus seemed to realize more about who Jesus was and what he had come to do than had any of his other disciples. What can we learn from this?

Like the woman who anointed Jesus, we can practice extravagant devotion. Her act was, we might say, over the top. Unless she was a wealthy woman, she was likely giving up for Jesus' sake the most valuable possession she had. We can safely assume that her great gift was motivated by her great love. How can we show such extravagant devotion to Jesus?

Like the woman who anointed Jesus, we can follow the best understanding we have. It is an open question whether the woman intended to anoint Jesus' body for his coming burial. But Jesus interpreted her act in that way, so that was what she was doing whether she fully realized it or not. Whatever she understood, she followed the best insight she had. Perhaps more importantly, she followed the best love she had. If we follow our best insight and our best love, how will we recognize and honor Jesus? How will our lifestyle be affected?

Like the woman who anointed Jesus, we can align our lives with the crucified Savior. Jesus affirmed that she had anointed him in preparation for his burial. In effect, then, she was participating in what he was going through. When Jesus said earlier, "All who want to come after me must say no to themselves, take up their cross, and follow me" (Mark 8:34), was this woman there to hear him? Either way, we are here to hear him and to observe what this woman did. How do we participate in the death of

Jesus? How do we live in ways that share in what Jesus did and in what this woman did?

What About Me?

• *What am I willing for my love for Jesus to cost me?* The woman who anointed Jesus did so at great cost to her finances and to her reputation. The ointment was costly, and her loving action prompted talk. What are we willing to sacrifice to show our love for Jesus?

• *Am I striking an appropriate balance between worshipping Christ and serving others?* The disciples questioned whether the woman's expensive gift should rather have been spent on the poor. Believers ponder similar questions today. How can we best live out the obligations of worship and service as two parts of the same reality?

• *What kind of legacy will I leave?* Just as Jesus said, this woman is still remembered today for her act of love for Jesus and her identification with his death. Will we be remembered for the way we took up our crosses and followed him?

Resources

R. Alan Culpepper, *Mark*, Smyth & Helwys Bible Commentary (Macon GA: Smyth & Helwys, 2007).

William L. Lane, "The Gospel of Mark," *The New International Commentary on the New Testament* (Grand Rapids MI: Eerdmans, 1974).

Donald Senior, *The Passion of Jesus in the Gospel of Mark* (Collegeville MN: Liturgical Press, 1984).

A MISSION
TO EMBRACE

Isaiah 61:1-3a; Mark 14:1-9

Introduction

1 Kings 18 recounts the battle between the prophet Elijah and the prophets of Baal. The writer of 1 Kings set that passage up as a colossal battle between God and Baal. God is the indisputable winner.

Our passage this lesson from Mark describes another colossal battle, though this one is much more subtle and understated. In Mark 14, a woman approaches Jesus while he is in the home of Simon the leper and anoints him with expensive ointment. That ointment was worth a year's salary for most workers of that day, so it was expensive indeed. Some of the chief priests and experts in the law, who were present and being their typical judgmental selves, scoffed at her silly extravagance. Jesus, though, defended her deed and praised her. He even saw her anointing as a final, gracious gift before his death.

Centuries before this woman anointed Jesus with her expensive perfume, the prophet in Isaiah 61 had foreseen a day when God would anoint a chosen messenger to bring good news to the poor, bind up the brokenhearted, proclaim release for the captives, bring liberation for prisoners, and announce the year of the Lord's favor. Jesus later stood in the synagogue in his hometown of Nazareth and declared that he was the fulfillment of that promise.

The woman's anointing gave Jesus the opportunity to teach something crucial about this new kingdom he had come to establish. Not only had he come to be the fulfillment of Isaiah 61, he had also come to teach people the meaning of the word "love," and this unnamed woman became the perfect example of what he had in mind.

This passage brings into focus two ways of relating to God and people: the way of religion, as practiced by the priests and experts in the law, and the way of grace, as practiced by this unnamed woman. As surely as Elijah and the prophets of Baal clashed on Mount Carmel, these two ways of approaching God clashed there in the home of Simon the leper. It is a battle well worth studying, and its outcome is more than shocking.

The Way of Religion

On one side in this battle were the religious leaders, who, Mark says, were plotting to seize Jesus and kill him. They had been hounding Jesus for days, finding fault with him and accusing him of various wrongdoings. In their eyes, everything Jesus did, even kind things such as healing the sick, were of the devil.

One of the most scathing passages in the New Testament is found in Matthew 23, in which Jesus fires back at these religious leaders and tells them precisely what he thinks of their religion. He fires seven "woes" at their brand of religion. When you analyze them, they describe four fatal flaws of the religion of the scribes and Pharisees. For that matter, they describe the four fatal flaws of any religious system.

First, *religion is overly concerned about appearances*. "Everything they do, they do to be noticed by others. They make extra-wide prayer bands for their arms and long tassels for their clothes. They love to sit in places of honor at banquets. They love to be greeted with honor in the markets and to be addressed as 'Rabbi'" (Matt 23:5-7). Jesus advocated praying, fasting, and giving in secret, but the religious leaders would have none of that. They wanted their piety noticed and applauded.

Second, *religion is blind to personal sin*. "How terrible it will be for you legal experts and Pharisees! Hypocrites! You clean the outside of the cup and plate, but inside they are full of violence and pleasure seeking. Blind Pharisee! First clean the inside of the cup so that the outside of the cup will be clean too" (Matt 23:25-26). Ironically, the religious leaders were experts at noticing and criticizing the sins of others. They were quick to see if someone violated some obscure law or failed to make a proper animal sacrifice. But they were completely blind to their own sin, their own legalistic, judgmental spirit.

Third, *religion emphasizes rules over people.* "You give to God a tenth of mint, dill, and cumin, but you forget about the more important matters of the Law: justice, peace, and faith. You ought to give a tenth but without forgetting about those more important matters" (Matt 23:23). The religious leaders had pinpointed 613 Old Testament laws that needed to be obeyed. Then there were interpretations of those laws and interpretations of the interpretations. They were drowning in minutiae and neglecting justice, peace, and faith.

Fourth, *religion places a heavy obligation on people.* "For they tie together heavy packs that are impossible to carry. They put them on the shoulders of others, but are unwilling to lift a finger to move them" (Matt 23:4). Religion is heavy, nitpicking, and life-sapping. It loads people down with laws and commandments. It tells people to believe this doctrine, assume this religious pose, perform this pious transaction, and God will bless them. But the whole process is draining and depressing.

When the religious leaders showed up at the home of Simon the leper, they brought all of that religious baggage with them. It was that religious baggage that made them want to seize and kill Jesus. And it was that religious baggage that made them criticize the woman for her extravagant gift of that precious ointment. Jesus was so anti-religion that they couldn't stand him. And the woman was so joyfully generous that they couldn't stand her, either.

So, there is no doubt that respectable religion was present that day in the home of Simon the leper. It hung in the air like a dark cloud, threatening to rain on anything or anyone that smacked of grace.

The Way of Grace

On the other side in this battle (though she never planned on being in a battle, I'm sure) was this woman, who embodied the way of grace. For people like the religious leaders, grace makes no sense at all, and it makes no sense for two obvious reasons:

First, *grace isn't logical*. The religious leaders were right in their assessment that the expensive perfume could have been used in a more logical, sensible way. It could have been sold and the money used to help the poor. Who can argue with that reasoning? Grace simply doesn't make sense. It is extravagant, and it usually arises out of a heart that is overflowing with joy and gratitude. Grace is irrationally generous.

Second, *grace isn't careful*. Frankly, this woman was making a fool of herself. It's as if she forgot her reputation, her image, and her role at the party. She made a scene and could have embarrassed both herself and Jesus—except that Jesus refused to be embarrassed by her. Grace typically forgets itself and gives itself in a foolish display of gratitude.

The religious leaders, schooled in the four rules of religion listed above, couldn't believe this woman was acting so crazy. She was adhering to exactly none of their four rules. She wasn't concerned about appearances. She wasn't concerned about their stringent definition of sin. She couldn't care less about their rules and regulations. And she wanted to lift a burden off of Jesus, not load him down with more burdens. Everything about this woman irritated the religious leaders, so it's no wonder they "scolded her" (Mark 14:5).

There they stood in Simon's house—the religious leaders, regal representatives of respectable religion, and the woman, a lonely representative of the way of grace. She was as outnumbered and outmanned as Elijah was that day on Mount Carmel.

But, as in that encounter on Mount Carmel, the winner of the battle was a big surprise.

And the Winner Is...

Let's let Jesus himself tell us who won this tussle. Which way is right: the way of religion or the way of grace? Jesus says,

> Leave her alone. Why do you make trouble for her? She has done a good thing for me. You always have the poor with you; and whenever you want, you can do something good for them. But you won't always have me. She has done what she could. She has anointed my body ahead of time for burial. I tell you

the truth that, wherever in the whole world the good news is announced, what she's done will also be told in memory of her. (Mark 14:6-9)

To put it simply, the woman won—at least in Jesus' eyes. Her way was the best way. Her gift was not foolish; it was a way of anointing Jesus' body for burial. Her gracious act at Simon's house would not be looked back on and laughed at. It would be looked back on and used as a model for how to relate to others. At least in Jesus' mind, she, and not the respectable religious leaders, was the role model we should follow.

But that's Jesus' thinking. Not everyone in that day—or in our day—agrees with him. The religion of the scribes and Pharisees has never gone away and is still thriving in our world and in our churches.

When it comes to our relationship to God, it just feels right to think that our destiny is in our hands and that we decide our fate with God by how many religious deeds we can do. The works system makes a lot more sense than the grace system. So to this day, religion "sells" better than grace. The notion that we can work our way to God's favor has always attracted a following.

When it comes to our relationship to people, it also feels right to relate to others the way the scribes and Pharisees did, to be logical and careful and give people what they deserve and nothing more. The old eye-for-an-eye ethic of the Old Testament, where we give back to people precisely what they give to us, is still the reigning ethic in human relationships. The woman's way of grace—of extravagant, irrational generosity—seems silly to the majority of people.

But, at least according to Jesus, the way of grace is the way to live. The winner of the subtle, understated battle in the home of Simon the leper was not the powerful, prestigious religious leaders, but this unnamed woman who had no power or prestige at all.

Conclusion

Two lessons ago, we began our Lenten study by looking at the great commandment in Mark 12:28-34. That passage was like a cool oasis in a desert of doctrinal confusion. In terms we could all understand, it gave us our marching orders. We must love God with all of our heart, mind, soul, and strength and love our neighbor as we love ourselves. In short, we are to focus on loving God and loving people.

This story about Jesus' anointing is a fine sequel to that previous lesson about the greatest commandment. It defines for us the meaning of the word "love." We are to love God because God has first loved us and redeemed us in Christ. Our love for God is in gratitude for God's love for us. And we are to love our neighbor with that same kind of gracious love. Freely we have received it from God, and freely we give it to our neighbors. Recipients of grace become bestowers of grace.

I suppose in studying this passage on the woman who anointed Jesus with the precious perfume, we are actually fulfilling its prophecy. Jesus said that wherever in the world the good news is announced, what she did would be told in memory of her. And here we are, 2,000 years after she lived and died, marveling at her gracious gift and using her as our role model.

May her ethic of gracious generosity become the ruling ethic in all of our relationships.

Notes

Notes

4

A MEAL
TO SHARE

Isaiah 25:6-10; Mark 14:13-16, 22-26

Central Question

How does the Lord's Supper strengthen my faith?

Scripture

Isaiah 25:6-10 On this mountain, the LORD of heavenly forces will prepare for all peoples a rich feast, a feast of choice wines, of select foods rich in flavor, of choice wines well refined. 7 He will swallow up on this mountain the veil that is veiling all peoples, the shroud enshrouding all nations. 8 He will swallow up death forever. The LORD God will wipe tears from every face; he will remove his people's disgrace from off the whole earth, for the LORD has spoken. 9 They will say on that day, "Look! This is our God, for whom we have waited—and he has saved us! This is the LORD, for whom we have waited; let's be glad and rejoice in his salvation!" 10 The LORD 's hand will indeed rest on this mountain. Moab will be trampled down as straw is trampled into manure.

Mark 14:13-16, 22-26 He sent two of his disciples and said to them, "Go into the city. A man carrying a water jar will meet you. Follow him. 14 Wherever he enters, say to the owner of the house, 'The teacher asks, Where is my guest room where I can eat the Passover meal with my disciples?' 15 He will show you a large room upstairs already furnished. Prepare for us there." 16 The disciples left, came into the city, found everything just as he had told them, and they prepared the Passover meal.... 22 While they were eating, Jesus took bread, blessed it, broke it, and gave it to them, and said, "Take; this is my body." 23 He took a cup, gave thanks, and gave it to them, and they all drank from it. 24 He said to them, "This is my blood of the covenant, which is poured out for many. 25 I assure you that I won't drink wine again until that day when I drink it in a new way in God's kingdom." 26 After singing songs of praise, they went out to the Mount of Olives.

Reflecting

The beloved pastor of my growing-up years would stand behind the Communion table as he was about to serve the Lord's Supper and say, "Now, we don't believe like some do that the bread and juice really are the body and blood of Christ." I understood what he was saying, but I found myself wishing he would spend less time talking about what we *didn't* believe about this special observance and more time talking about what we *did* believe about it.

I can still remember a Communion service in which I participated a few years ago. I did not have leadership responsibilities, so I was able to give myself over to the experience. As someone broke the loaf of bread, tears began to run down my face. As I went forward to receive a piece of the bread and dip it in the cup before consuming it, it was all I could do not to sob.

> When has your observance of Communion moved you to deep emotion? What factors (personal or liturgical) led you to experience Communion this way?

Something real was happening. Something real does happen. Somehow, the act of eating the bread and drinking the cup brings healing and strength. That it happens is perhaps more important than how it happens. At any rate, we can say this much with confidence: it happens when we participate because, in participating, we share in what Jesus did and does for us.

Studying

The Lord's Supper strengthens our faith by leading us to look back and to look ahead, even as we fully live in the present moment. We can draw that conclusion from the way in which Mark presents the original Lord's Supper that occurred on the Passover evening the day before Jesus was crucified. For Christians, the commemoration of that Passover became Maundy or Holy Thursday, the night that Jesus shared his last meal with his disciples.

Mark's presentation shows how the events of that night should have encouraged the disciples who were present to look back and to look forward even as they experienced what was happening on that night. It also should have encouraged Mark's readers, to whom he was writing some forty years after these events. Finally, it should encourage us to consider the implications of these great events for their and for our discipleship.

Mark's account of the Last Supper looks back. It looks back, first of all, to the original Passover that was observed by the Hebrews on the night before they escaped Egyptian captivity. The story of that first Passover is told in Exodus 12. On the night the first-born in Egypt were killed, each Hebrew household killed a lamb, spread some of its blood on the doorposts of their houses, and then ate the lamb along with unleavened bread and bitter herbs. The Lord said, "Whenever I see the blood, I'll pass over you" (Exod 12:13). The day of Passover was to "be a day of remembering." The Hebrews were to "observe it as a festival to the LORD...in every generation as a regulation for all time" (Exod 12:14).

God's instructions for the observance of the Passover are found in Exodus 12:1-15.

So Jesus and his disciples were, along with many other Jews, gathered in Jerusalem for the festival, doing what they were supposed to do, which caused them to look back on what God had done to deliver God's people in the past.

Mark's presentation of the Last Supper also looks back to the event when a Jewish crowd of 5,000 ate all the bread they wanted and had twelve basketsful left over (6:30-44) and back to the event when a Gentile crowd of 4,000 ate all the bread they wanted and had seven basketsful left over (Mark 8:1-10). "The supper in 14:22-25 is, therefore, the third in a series of messianic meals in the Gospel" (Senior, 58), since the two mass feedings are meant to signify, among other things, that Jesus has brought about a foretaste, so to speak, of the anticipated great messianic banquet to which texts such as Isaiah 25:6-10 pointed and to which, Mark's presentation stresses, all people are invited.

Mark's presentation of the Last Supper not only looks back. It also looks ahead. It looks ahead, first, to the crucifixion of Jesus.

The crucifixion is the event to which the entire Gospel has been pointing. The Gospel opens with the words "The beginning of the good news about Jesus Christ, God's Son" (Mark 1:1), but no human being recognizes Jesus by that title until he dies on the cross (15:39). Three times Jesus tells his disciples that his execution is coming (9:27-38;10:32-34) and all three times, they confirm through words and actions that they don't understand or don't accept what Jesus is saying. In the first instance, Peter accosts Jesus in his vehement denial of Jesus' words. In the second, the disciples immediately argue about who among them is the greatest. In the third, James and John ask for positions of authority in Jesus' kingdom.

Now, though, Jesus breaks bread and passes it among his disciples and says, "This is my body," and passes a cup of wine among them and says, "This is my blood of the covenant, which is poured out for many" (Mark 14:22, 24). Those actions clearly point toward Jesus' death on the cross.

Jesus said that the cup of which we partake is "my blood of the covenant" (v. 24). This is the only time that the word "covenant" appears in Mark's Gospel (Boring, 391). It recalls the covenant that God established with the Hebrews following the first Passover and the promise of the new covenant in Jeremiah 31:31-34 (Senior, 60-61)—a promise that was fulfilled through the crucifixion of Jesus.

Jesus also said that when we eat the bread and drink the cup we receive his body and blood. This eating and drinking point us toward the reality that to follow Christ is to share in—to participate in—his

> Therefore, if you were raised with Christ, look for the things that are above where Christ is sitting at God's right side. Think about the things above and not things on earth. You died, and your life is hidden with Christ in God. When Christ, who is your life, is revealed, then you also will be revealed with him in glory. (Col 3:1-4)

death. According to Borg and Crossan, "It was by participation *with* Jesus and, even more, *in* Jesus that his followers were to pass through death to resurrection" (119). To share in the Lord's Supper teaches us that to follow Christ is to share in his death. It also gives us the strength to do so.

Mark's presentation of the Last Supper also looks forward to the coming fulfilled kingdom. "I assure you," Jesus says, "that I won't drink wine again until that day when I drink it in a new way in God's kingdom" (v. 25). The Old Testament prophets encouraged the people to look forward to a day when a great messianic banquet would take place. A good example of this hope is in Isaiah 25:6, where the prophet promises a rich feast of choice food and wine. When that time comes, Isaiah continues, God will "swallow up death forever" (v. 8).

It is to such wine and to such a kingdom that Jesus refers. The resurrection that will follow Jesus' crucifixion points toward that fulfilled kingdom.

The disciples' recollection of the first Lord's Supper would have eventually strengthened their faith by leading them to look back in remembrance and to look forward in hope. Mark's presentation of this key event strengthened the faith of the Christians to whom Mark's Gospel was originally addressed. It also strengths the faith of all the disciples who have come after them—including us. It leads us to look back to the first Lord's Supper and forward to the coming messianic banquet. It can have this effect because those first disciples participated in the original experience, and because we today participate in its regular reenactment in the celebration of Holy Communion—and because we participate in a cross-centered life of following Jesus.

Understanding

The Last Supper that Jesus shared with his disciples was not an isolated incident. It was part and parcel of the kind of life Jesus had determined to live. It was a time of worship, and Jesus had been faithful to the worship practices of his ancestors. It was a time of fellowship, and Jesus had been intentional about building fellowship with other people and especially with his disciples.

Most importantly, though, it was a time of service and sacrifice, and Jesus' entire life was about service and sacrifice. During the Supper, Jesus, in the last hours of his life, tried to give his followers something that would help them. The Lord's Supper pointed toward and assumed Jesus' impending crucifixion and so served to try (again) to help the disciples understand what was coming. It also served to give them a practice that would, on the other side of the crucifixion, help them remember and make sense of what had happened.

How does the Lord's Supper proclaim the good news of Christ's saving work? How does it "make sense of what happened" in the cross and resurrection?

Beyond Jesus' crucifixion and resurrection, all the disciples except Judas came to understand and participate in his kind of life. They faithfully took up their crosses and followed him. They were obedient to God's call on their lives and gave of themselves until they had nothing left to give. They were joined to Jesus in his life and death.

It isn't hard to imagine how meaningful their future observances of the Lord's Supper would be as they shared in it as a part of their overarching practice of giving themselves away for the sake of living and proclaiming God's good news.

Now here we are, two millennia after these events. Do we share in the Lord's Supper in the midst of leading cross-centered lives? How can we move further toward such Christlike living? We need the strength that the Supper gives us by reminding us of what God did and does for us in Christ and in reminding us of Christ's ongoing presence with us. We need its strength to help us live the life we are called in Christ to live.

What About Me?

• *What does sharing in the Lord's Supper mean to me?* Is it more than a mere ritual? If not, how can I experience the Lord's Supper as Christ intended? What distractions do I need to put away? What spiritual preparation should I make? When I reflect on the meaning of this sacred act, what images come to mind?

• *Am I leading the kind of life that participation in the Lord's Supper can strengthen me in living?* Am I living a life of love, service, obedience, and sacrifice? If I am living a life that is based on self-fulfillment rather than self-emptying, can I expect the Lord's Supper to be a strengthening experience for me?

• *Does my participation in the Lord's Supper point me toward God's great future?* The kingdom of God is going to be consummated and the purposes of God are going to be fulfilled. Jesus' words about not drinking wine again until he drinks it "in a new way in God's kingdom" (Mark 14:25) point us toward that great future. Does the Lord's Supper give us encouragement for the present by reminding us of our hope for the future?

Resources

Marcus J. Borg and John Dominic Crossan, *The Last Week: What the Gospels Really Teach About Jesus's Final Days in Jerusalem* (New York: HarperOne, 2006).

M. Eugene Boring, "Mark: A Commentary," *The New Testament Library* (Louisville KY: Westminster John Knox, 2006).

Donald Senior, *The Passion of Jesus in the Gospel of Mark* (Collegeville MN: Liturgical Press, 1984).

A MEAL
TO SHARE

Isaiah 25:6-10; Mark 14:13-16, 22-26

Introduction

When my children were young, they went through a time when they were enamored with "Magic Eye" books. I have to confess that I became enamored with them, too.

These books had pages of 3D pictures that had hidden images embedded in them. If you stared at the picture long enough at just the right angle, suddenly the image would appear. But sometimes you had to look at it intently for a minute or two for anything to happen. A quick glance at one of the "Magic Eye" pictures yielded nothing. You really had to focus on it to see the hidden image.

We Christians are often guilty, I'm afraid, of just glancing at our faith. We sing the hymns without paying attention to the words. We hear the sermons without giving them careful, critical thought. We read the popular biblical stories, such as the prodigal son and the Good Samaritan, but they are so familiar to us we're on autopilot when we read them. In fact, "autopilot" might be a good way to describe our faith. We've been there and done that so many times that our faith has lost its power to move us.

That been-there-done-that syndrome can certainly apply to the Lord's Supper. Some of us have received the Lord's Supper so many times we've forgotten what it is supposed to mean to us, or do in us. So, maybe what we need to do now, as we study this passage from Mark where Jesus transforms the Passover feast into the Lord's Supper, is stare at it for a while until the picture becomes clear to us. Hidden in this simple symbol of eating the bread and drinking the cup are some profound truths about the past, the present, and the future.

The Past: A Remembrance That Makes Us Grateful

The Lord's Supper is, first of all, a time of remembering. Mark doesn't include Jesus' statement about remembering in his version of the story, but Luke does: "Do this in remembrance of me" (Luke 22:19). In the passage we typically quote when we celebrate the Supper, the command to remember appears twice: "This is my body, which is for you; do this to remember me" (1 Cor 11:24). "This cup is the new covenant in my blood. Every time you drink it, do this to remember me" (1 Cor 11:25).

From the time Jesus first transformed the Passover feast into the Lord's Supper, Christians have been receiving the bread and cup and using them to jog their memories. Every time we celebrate the Lord's Supper, we remember his body broken for us and his blood shed on our behalf.

Those disciples who were there at the first Lord's Supper were probably not shocked at all that Jesus could give them a symbol to remind them of his death. As Jews, the disciples were schooled in symbols designed to provoke sacred memories. They had festivals, feasts, and phylacteries all for the purpose of helping them remember their past. And they had an abundance of sacred monuments and shrines to remind them of their history as God's people. If something significant happened to the ancient Israelites, they erected a stone, established a festival, or composed a story to commemorate it.

When Jesus took the bread and wine, he was doing what Jews have always done: create symbols as tools of remembrance. And every time we receive the Lord's Supper, we do what those first disciples did. We remember Christ's body and his blood, and we express that we are grateful for his death.

Every time we eat the bread and drink the cup we celebrate the glorious truth of 1 John 4:10: "This is love: it is not that we loved God but that he loved us and sent his Son as the sacrifice that deals with our sins." The Lord's Supper reminds us that God loved us *first*. Everything we do in our lives is in response to a love we neither earned nor deserved. All we can do is be grateful *for* it and live in celebration *of* it.

There is a rhythm to a life of faith, and the first note is gratitude. All that we do in our Christian discipleship must come from a grateful heart. We have been loved. We have been died for. And so we preach, sing, give, teach, write, paint, and parent in response to a love that proved itself on a cross.

We should never receive the Lord's Supper without whispering a prayer of gratitude for God's love.

The Present: A Reminder That Gives Us Purpose

The Lord's Supper also has implications for the present. Not only does this observance enable us to look back, remember Jesus' death, and be grateful, it also clarifies for us our purpose in life. Since we're all forgetful, and since the world is so loud and demanding, anything we can do to keep first things first is helpful. If receiving the bread and cup can refocus our attention on our real purpose in life, maybe we ought to celebrate the Lord's Supper every day!

I used to have a hand-stitched plaque on the wall that read, "Only One Life; 'Twill Soon Be Past; Only What's Done for Christ Will Last." The sentiment seemed a bit shallow to me—like something you might see on a bumper sticker—so I took it down.

But the thrust of that statement is true. I should be investing my life in the things that matter. And if he were alive today, the Apostle Paul would probably have no problem with that plaque. After all, he told the Corinthians, "I had made up my mind not to think about anything while I was with you except Jesus Christ, and to preach him as crucified" (1 Cor 2:2). That was Paul's version of "Only what's done for Christ will last."

When we receive the Lord's Supper, we Christians are invited to remember our calling. Above all else, we are followers of Christ. Before we are Americans, Baptists, Republicans, or Cowboys fans, we are followers of Jesus Christ. We are to learn about him, pray in his name, steep our lives in his teachings, and be his ambassadors everywhere we go. The Lord's Supper reminds us who we are and *Whose* we are.

It also reminds us that others have chosen to follow Christ, too. When Jesus first instituted the Lord's Supper, he did it among his friends in a community meal. They celebrated the Supper together, as brothers in Christ. Eventually, they must have looked back on that occasion and taken courage from it. They were part of a community, and they all had found their purpose in Christ. They were not solitary saints, alone and frightened. They were part of a body of people who had found the same purpose they had found.

So, the next time we celebrate the Lord's Supper, let's remember our purpose in life. It is not to make money, get promotions, or impress our neighbors. It is to be Christ to the world. And the next time we celebrate the Lord's Supper, let's look around and be grateful that other fine folks have made that same declaration. They, too, have found life in Christ.

We should never approach the Table without whispering a prayer recommitting ourselves to the way of Jesus.

The Future: A Reunion That Gives Us Hope

In Mark 14:25, Jesus says, "I assure you that I won't drink wine again until that day when I drink it in a new way in God's kingdom." Paul's version of the story also looks to the future: "Every time you eat this bread and drink this cup, you broadcast the death of the Lord until he comes" (1 Cor 11:26). Mark describes Jesus drinking wine in a new way in God's kingdom. Paul has him coming again. Both use the Lord's Supper to anticipate a reunion with Christ that is full of hope.

There is little doubt that when Jesus first spoke these words to his followers, they didn't have a clue what he was talking about. They couldn't imagine him dying, much less being resurrected to drink wine with them in a new kingdom or coming again in glory. Only in retrospect, after the cross and resurrection, did what he said in the upper room make sense to them.

Since we live on the far side of the cross and resurrection, we can better understand the import of his words. When we receive the bread and cup, we are supposed to anticipate a future reunion with Christ. He doesn't give us all of the details (and we would love to know them) but he does at least hint at a glorious reunion in the future.

Our local newspaper has a weekly feature that focuses on a high school athlete. These students have obviously been given some questions ahead of time and asked to respond to them. One of the questions always included in the interview is, "If you could have dinner with any four people in history, who would they be?"

As you might imagine, these teenagers have given a variety of answers to that question. Some would like to have dinner with Justin Bieber, Lady Gaga, or rappers whose names I can't remember. Others have opted for sports heroes such as Babe Ruth, Michael Jordan, or Chris Evert. A few of those high school athletes put Jesus on their list.

They know, of course, that they are answering a hypothetical question. But, according to our passage for this lesson, having dinner with Jesus is not as far-fetched as it might seem. Jesus promises to meet his disciples in a reunion in God's kingdom.

Don't you know that those men in that upper room would cling to that promise in the days to come? When Jesus died on the cross, when the incredible resurrection happened, when they faced persecution for their allegiance to Christ, and when bad things happened to them that made no sense at all, they remembered what Jesus had said, and they found hope. They would see him again, have dinner with him again, and all would be well. On the other side of all of their problems and questions, there was a promise from Jesus to meet them for dinner.

That future dimension is a crucial part of the Lord's Supper. We never receive it without casting our eyes to the future. Jesus is coming again. He will drink wine in a new way in God's kingdom. So, beyond all of our fears, all will be well. He's got it all under control.

We should never receive the Lord's Supper without whispering a prayer that celebrates the empty tomb and the promise of a reunion with our risen Lord.

Conclusion

Since my children are now grown and it's been a long time since we looked at those "Magic Eye" books, I googled them to see if those books are still around. Sure enough, they still are. The website even had some 3D pictures to gaze at, so I spent several minutes staring at my computer screen.

I'm sad to report that I never saw the hidden image in the picture. The website said it's harder to see the image on a computer screen, so maybe that was my problem. But I stared and stared, and nothing happened.

Let's hope that doesn't happen to us as we try to refocus on the meaning of the Lord's Supper. Receiving the Supper can be more than a tired ritual at church. It can be more than a 2,000-year-old tradition that has outlived its usefulness. And it can be more than a time to try to explain to our young kids and grand-kids why they don't get to participate. The Lord's Supper can be a symbol of Jesus' death that fills us with gratitude, purpose, and hope.

I pray that we will all get the picture.

Notes

Notes

A PRAYER
TO PRAY

Psalm 141; Mark 14:32-42

Central Question

How can I pray when my path is too hard?

Scripture

Psalm 141 I cry out to you, LORD: Come to me—quickly! Listen to my voice when I cry out to you! 2 Let my prayer stand before you like incense; let my uplifted hands be like the evening offering. 3 Set a guard over my mouth, LORD; keep close watch over the door that is my lips. 4 Don't let my heart turn aside to evil things so that I don't do wicked things with evildoers, so I don't taste their delicacies. 5 Instead, let the righteous discipline me; let the faithful correct me! Let my head never reject that kind of fine oil, because my prayers are always against the deeds of the wicked. 6 Their leaders will fall from jagged cliffs, but my words will be heard because they are pleasing. 7 Our bones have been scattered at the mouth of the grave, just like when the ground is broken up and plowed. 8 But my eyes are on you, my Lord God. I take refuge in you; don't let me die! 9 Protect me from the trap they've set for me; protect me from the snares of the evildoers. 10 Let the wicked fall into their own nets—all together!— but let me make it through safely.

Mark 14:32-42 Jesus and his disciples came to a place called Gethsemane. Jesus said to them, "Sit here while I pray." 33 He took Peter, James, and John along with him. He began to feel despair and was anxious. 34 He said to them, "I'm very sad. It's as if I'm dying. Stay here and keep alert." 35 Then he went a short distance farther and fell to the ground. He prayed that, if possible, he might be spared the time of suffering. 36 He said, "Abba, Father, for you all things are possible. Take this cup of suffering away from me. However—not what I want but what you want." 37 He came and found them sleeping. He said to Peter, "Simon, are you asleep? Couldn't you stay alert for one hour? 38 Stay alert and pray so that you won't give in to temptation. The spirit is eager, but the flesh is weak." 39 Again, he left them and prayed, repeating the same words. 40 And, again, when he came back, he found them sleeping, for they couldn't keep their eyes open, and they didn't know how to respond to him. 41 He came a third time and said to them, "Will you sleep and rest all night? That's enough! The time has come for the Human One to be betrayed into the hands of sinners. 42 Get up! Let's go! Look, here comes my betrayer."

Reflecting

In the preface to a 1962 reprint of his 1915 classic *The Meaning of Prayer*, Harry Emerson Fosdick noted the circumstances that helped give birth to the book. He said,

> I was then a young minister in my first parish, still bearing the scars of a nervous breakdown which I had suffered in seminary days. In fighting my way through that devastating experience prayer had become an indispensable resource. So I preached a series of sermons, presenting such insight as I had gained into prayer's meaning. (iii)

It is good to learn about prayer from those who have learned to pray through the hard times of life. From the Christian perspective, it is good to learn about prayer from those whose hard times have come in the course of, and even because of, their commitment to the call of God on their lives.

Jesus prayed regularly and often. At times, he spent all night praying. His early followers remembered his prayer life and left us accounts of it in the Gospels. Given that Jesus' disciples faced persecution and death for following him, they no doubt looked back with great appreciation on the time that Jesus spent praying in Gethsemane on the night he was betrayed.

Given that Mark's audience was undergoing persecution as well, they were no doubt grateful for Jesus' honest expression of his conflict over the trial he faced. In Jesus' prayer, we too find a vital resource on which to draw as we face our own struggles to be faithful in trying times.

Studying

As we examine this lesson's Gospel text, it might be helpful to pair the central question with its opposite: how can I *not* pray when my path is too hard? Indeed, in our text we are confronted with two opposing models of how to deal with stressful situations: the one offered by Jesus and the one offered by Peter, James, and John. Both models are encouraging, one as an approach to life toward which to grow and the other as an approach to life from which to grow away.

Mark's introduction to this passage has us thinking about the possibility of faltering in our faith. After the Passover meal, Jesus and his disciples go to the Mount of Olives. There, Jesus warns them that they are going to fail him and flee from him. When Peter insists that he will not do so, Jesus tells him that he will deny his teacher three times that very night. All of them insist that they will not deny Jesus (Mark 14:27-31).

> When has overconfidence caused you trouble? When has it caused you trouble in your spiritual life?

Perhaps the disciples have an opportunity to escape the shame of denial and desertion if they will but listen to Jesus and follow his example of prayer. They come to Gethsemane, which is transformed by Christ's presence into a place of prayer. Jesus tells most of his disciples to "Sit here while I pray" (v. 32). Although Jesus doesn't tell them to pray, it is reasonable to conclude that Jesus expected them to share in his season of prayer. (In Luke 22:39-40, Jesus does tell all of the disciples to pray at this point.)

Jesus leads his inner circle of Peter, James, and John away from the rest of the disciples. He shares with them the deep feelings of despair and sadness he is experiencing (vv. 33-34). Previously, those same three disciples had accompanied him to the mountain where he was transfigured (9:2-13). There, they witnessed clear evidence of Jesus' divinity. Now, they witness clear evidence of his humanity (Boring, 397).

When Jesus tells the three disciples "I'm very sad. It's as if I'm dying" (v. 34) and then falls on the ground to pour his heart out to his Father, he does so out of the real experience of suffering he is undergoing. He also acts out of a long-standing tradition of lament. Psalm 141 offers an example of such an experience of prayer. Note generally the tone of the psalm and specifically the way these lines remind us of Jesus' situation: "But my eyes are on you, my LORD God. I take refuge in you; don't let me die! Protect me from the trap they've set for me; protect me from the snares of the evildoers" (Ps 141:8-9). Jesus does not quote these lines, and there is no way to know if the words of this or any other psalm were in his mind as he prayed in Gethsemane. Still, he gives us a great gift in affirming the appropriateness of using such strong, pleading language—language given to us in the biblical psalms of lament— in the prayers that we offer in desperate times and circumstances.

> The lament is the psalmist's cry when in great distress he has nowhere to turn but to God.... Though the mood of the lament is generally melancholic, there are one or two moments when the psalmist makes clear his basic trust in God. (Longman, 26, 28)

Some other words in Psalm 141 help us to think about the disciples' Gethsemane experience: "Don't let my heart turn aside to evil things so that I don't do wicked things with evildoers" (v. 4). In other words, the one praying the psalm prays not to give in to temptation. When Jesus first leaves Peter, James, and John to go off by himself to pray, he tells them, "Keep alert" (Mark 14:34), an instruction which could have the double meaning of watching out for those who were coming to arrest Jesus and to keep alert against the temptations that the unfolding events would bring to them (Culpepper, 501). When Jesus comes back the first time to check on the three disciples and finds them sleeping, he says to Peter, "Pray so that you won't give in to temptation" (v. 38).

In Luke's version, Jesus says this to all of the disciples (Luke 22:40, 46).

Unlike Matthew and Luke, Mark never records Jesus instructing his disciples with the words of the Model Prayer (the "Lord's Prayer"). But the instruction he gives them to pray so they won't enter into temptation reminds us of the petition "Lead us not into temptation" (Matt 6:13, KJV; Luke 11:4, KJV). Such a prayer is necessary in our ongoing struggle to be faithful.

During his first check-in with the three disciples, Jesus also says to Peter, "The spirit is eager, but the flesh is weak" (v. 38). It is difficult to determine whether Jesus refers to the human spirit or to the Holy Spirit. If the former, then he speaks of a struggle between the "spiritual" and "physical" components of a person. If the latter, he speaks of weak humans needing the help of God's Spirit to persevere under pressure. It seems best to opt for "Holy Spirit" (Lane, 520; Boring, 400). Jews tended to think of a person as a unified whole, which would argue against reference to the human spirit as a separate entity here.

Furthermore, in context, Jesus is praying for divine help—the help that comes from God's Spirit. The idea of an eager or willing spirit may be inspired by Psalm 51:12, where "willing spirit" may be poetically linked to the phrase "holy spirit" in Psalm 51:11. The disciples needed the help of God's Spirit if they were going to avoid the temptation that would lead to their failing Jesus.

Jesus' prayer in the garden is as much a model prayer for us as is the Lord's Prayer. He prays to his "Abba" (Mark 14:36), a very personal Aramaic word for "Father." He affirms the power of God to do anything. He asks for the "cup of suffering" to be taken from him (v. 36). Finally, he submits to the will of his Father. After so praying, Jesus resolutely gets up to face what is coming (vv. 41-42).

Jesus' way of praying made him ready to confront anything. The disciples' way of not praying made them ready to confront nothing.

Understanding

Pondering some vital questions will help us to better understand this story of Jesus and his disciples in Gethsemane.

First, what was Jesus' attitude toward Peter, James, and John in light of their failure to keep alert? His concern for them is evident in his continual checking on them. The first time, he chastises and encourages Simon. The second time, he says something but we aren't told what—only that they didn't know what to say to him. This might lead us to conclude that he expressed disappointment in them. The third time, he tells them it's time to get up and face what has to be faced. While Jesus had earlier told his disciples that they would desert him, he seems to have wanted them to learn that the way to deal with the stress of danger and testing was to stay alert and to pray. At the end, he was concerned that they had to face their enemies with him but without sharing his readiness. How important is it that we stay ready for whatever may come?

Second, what does Jesus' prayer teach us about how to pray? Jesus prayed that the cup of suffering that he was about to drink would pass from him. But he also said that he wanted what his Father wanted. He could not help but be concerned about what he was about to go through, but his main concern was that God's great purposes be carried out and that his life and death be used in that fulfillment. How important is it that we pray for God's will to be done?

Third, was Jesus' prayer answered? He asked that the cup of suffering pass from him. It didn't. But when it came time to face what had to be done, he was able to face it courageously and resolutely. So, was Jesus' prayer not answered or was it answered in a way that went above and beyond his request? How important is it that we give some thought to what constitutes answered prayer?

What About Me?

• *How prepared am I to deal with challenges that come because of my faithfulness to Christ?* Rest assured, if we try to lead lives that reflect the attitudes and actions of Jesus, we will face trying times. Being faithful to who we are in Christ can be difficult. Are we taking steps to let God's Spirit grow a spirit in us that can withstand the pressure?

• *How will I respond to Jesus' concern that I keep alert and ready?* It matters to him. Are we learning how to keep ourselves attuned and alert to what is going on within and around us so that we can be ready to face whatever comes?

• *When I pray "Thy will be done," what do I mean?* Or do I mean it at all? How can we grow in our understanding of God's will while confessing that we can never fully know it? How do we grow beyond wanting what we want to wanting what God wants? How do we keep from confusing what we want with what God wants?

Resource

M. Eugene Boring, "Mark: A Commentary," *The New Testament Library* (Louisville KY: Westminster John Knox, 2006).

R. Alan Culpepper, *Mark*, Smyth & Helwys Bible Commentary (Macon GA: Smyth & Helwys, 2007).

Harry Emerson Fosdick, *The Meaning of Prayer* (New York: Association, 1962).

William L. Lane, "The Gospel of Mark," *The New International Commentary on the New Testament* (Grand Rapids MI: Eerdmans, 1974).

Tremper Longman III, *How to Read the Psalms* (Downers Grove IL: InterVarsity, 1988).

A PRAYER
TO PRAY

Psalm 141; Mark 14:32-42

Introduction

Years ago, I visited a man in the hospital. He was the father of a member of our church. Though I had met the man before, I didn't really know him. But because I was a good friend of his son's, I wanted to see him and offer my prayers and support.

When I entered his room, I quickly realized the situation was more serious than I knew. My friend's father, in fact, was dying. His wife and a few family members were by his bed, and he was whispering his final words of love to them.

Of all the pastoral visits I've made through the years, that is one of the most memorable because I remember feeling so out of place. I barely knew the man. I shouldn't have been part of the inner circle of people privy to his dying words. I felt like an intruder and remember offering just a brief word of encourage-ment to the family and then slipping out the door. That occasion was so private, personal, and sacred, I felt I didn't belong there.

I have something of that same feeling when I read about Jesus in the garden of Gethsemane. This passage is so private, personal, and sacred, I almost want to turn my eyes away and slip out the door. It is so intimate and painful, I don't want to try to pull some inane "lessons for life" from it.

As we come to this last lesson from Mark, let's quietly and respectfully look at Jesus in the garden. Though we are familiar with this passage and it seems normal to us, it would not have seemed normal at all to a first-century Jew. Any Jew of that day, schooled in the messianic hopes of the nation of Israel, would not have believed this was happening to the Messiah.

Man of Sorrow

In particular, three facets of the Gethsemane experience would have shocked a typical first-century Jew. First, *he or she would have been shocked by the anguish Jesus experienced.*

Typical first-century Jews would have expected the Messiah to come in pomp and splendor and to return Israel to a place of prominence and power. They certainly would not have expected to hear that the Messiah "began to feel despair and was anxious" (Mark 14:33). They would not have expected the Messiah to be arrested like a common criminal. And, most shocking of all, they would not have expected the Messiah to be crucified between two thieves on a hill outside of Jerusalem.

Though there are passages in the Old Testament that predict a suffering servant kind of Messiah, the Jews of the first century typically ignored them in favor of a conquering king kind of Messiah, like King David. They were looking for a political leader, anointed by God.

We sometimes shake our head in amazement at the ignorance and blindness of Jesus' first disciples. We hear about them wanting to be prominent in his kingdom, for example, and wonder how they could have been so clueless. Why didn't they see Jesus for who he was? How could they have been so blind?

They could be so blind because they were typical first-century Jews, raised to believe certain things about the Messiah. Since Jesus wasn't a conquering king kind of Messiah, they didn't understand him at all. They expected him to be the conquering king, and they saw themselves as future cabinet members in his regime. But talking to children? Befriending sinners? Washing feet? Anguishing in a garden? Dying on a cross? None of that made sense to them, and they misunderstood him all the way to Calvary.

Mark makes it clear, though, that Jesus was suffering terribly in the garden: "I'm very sad. It's as if I am dying" (14:34). He knew how horrible it was to be crucified. He didn't want to go through that experience any more than you or I would want to go through that experience. So, he asked God to take this cup of suffering away from him.

Of course, this was not to be. He had to endure the agony of the garden, followed by the agony of a trumped-up trial, followed by the agony of a death on a Roman cross. No first-century Jew could have seen this coming for the long-expected Messiah.

We humans have spent a good deal of time trying to figure out why bad things happen to good people. So far, we've come up with very few satisfying answers. But ever since Jesus, we at least know this: God identifies with us in our suffering. God, in the person of Jesus, has walked a mile in our shoes.

Any time we face our own version of the garden of Gethsemane or our own version of the cross, we at least know that Someone has been there before us.

Unanswered Prayer

Second, *Jews of the first century would have been shocked that the Messiah's prayer was not answered.* Mark tells us that Jesus prayed, "Abba, Father, for you all things are possible. Take this cup of suffering away from me. However—not what I want but what you want" (14:36). If Jesus truly was the Messiah, wouldn't God grant his every request? Couldn't Jesus ask for anything and know that God would give it to him? One would think so. The Jews of the first century would have been incredulous at the notion that God would say no to the promised Messiah.

But that's precisely what happens in this passage. Jesus asks God to deliver him from the agony of the cross, but the cross happens anyway. It's as if Jesus' prayer in the garden got snagged on a tree limb and never made it to heaven. Either that, or worse, his prayer *does* make it to heaven, and God chooses to ignore it.

If we humans have spent a good deal of time wrestling with the issue of bad things happening to good people, we have also spent a good deal of time wrestling with the issue of unanswered prayer. How many times have we prayed diligently for something, only to feel as if our prayer bumped up against the ceiling and never got to heaven? Or worse, that it *did* get to heaven, and God ignored it.

There is, of course, one request that always gets answered, and it is the one at the end of Jesus' prayer: "However—not what I want but what you want" (14:36). Jesus wanted to escape the agony of the cross, but maybe that's not what God wanted. He put himself in the hands of a loving "Abba" whose sovereignty could be trusted without question.

I know what *I* want. I want my sick friends always to get well. I want my own physical problems to vanish. I want to be healthy, wealthy, and wise, for life to be full of fun and adventure. But I am not God, and so I need to pray like Jesus. I need to trust the sovereignty of God, even when I don't understand it.

Like the question of good people having to suffer, the question of unanswered prayer rises there in the garden. When we pray and nothing seems to happen, we at least know that Someone has been there before us.

Sleepy Friends

Third, *first-century Jews would have been shocked that the Messiah was deserted by his friends.* Mark tells us that Jesus went to his disciples three times. He doesn't tell us why Jesus went to them, but it's fair to assume, I think, that he needed companionship and comfort in his time of distress. He needed his friends to be with him as he faced death. It is a sad, pitiful picture Mark gives us here: a soon-to-be-dying man whose friends are not available to him in his suffering. For the Jews, it would have been an incomprehensible picture. They could not have envisioned the promised Messiah with no one to care for him.

Here's the third dilemma we have to wrestle with as we look at Jesus in the garden. How do we deal with people who have failed us? How can we live in a world where family members and friends so consistently drop the ball? As the old saying goes, with friends like these, who needs enemies?

When people used to ask me how I liked being a pastor, I would tell them (jokingly, of course) that being a pastor would be a great job if it wasn't for the people. The people in my churches were capable of anger, pettiness, bickering, jealousy, and getting all bent out of shape over trivial issues. They were also capable of love, kindness, generosity, humor, and grace.

In short, the people in my churches were a mixed bag, just like those disciples of Jesus nodding off in the garden of Gethsemane. They were his greatest joy—and his deepest disappointment.

We are all in the same boat Jesus was in. Our family and friends are our greatest source of encouragement and support. They are also our greatest source of irritation and distress. So what shall we do? Embrace them with open arms so we can be loved? Or flee from them as fast as we can so we can find peace? Which shall it be: engagement or seclusion?

However we choose to answer that question, ours is an age-old predicament, the same one Jesus faced in the garden. People will delight us, and people will destroy us. Sometimes, in our time of need, they will rise up and give us hope. And sometimes, in our time of need, they will fall asleep and leave us in despair.

But know this: when we wrestle with the dilemma of personal relationships and when we feel betrayed by friends, Someone has been there before us.

Conclusion

Seldom will we find in eleven verses of Scripture such a poignant microcosm of our greatest struggles. As Jesus came to the end of his life and had to grapple with the possibility of the cross, he also had to grapple with three of the biggest questions of human existence. They are questions that you and I still grapple with today:

• Why do good people have to suffer? More to the point, why do *I* have to suffer?
• Why doesn't God answer prayer? More to the point, why doesn't God answer *my* prayer?
• Why are people such a pain? More to the point, why are the people in *my* life such a pain?

If we gaze at Jesus long enough there in the garden of Gethsemane, those three questions come into focus. We see him not as a conquering king, full of pomp and splendor. We see him, instead, as a fellow human being. We see him as a young man who didn't want to die, who beseeched God to take the away the cross, and who needed the love and support of his friends.

As we come to the end of this unit from the Gospel of Mark, I want to jump, ironically, to a word associated not with Jesus' death but with his birth. In Isaiah 7:14, the prophet writes, "Therefore, the Lord will give you a sign. The young woman is pregnant and is about to give birth to a son, and she will name him Immanuel."

Immanuel means "God with us," and it is the word that best describes that scene in the garden of Gethsemane. There in that garden, God identified fully with our plight as human beings. In the person of Jesus, God wrestled with the very issues we wrestle with today. In the person of Jesus, God became one of us and faced the same struggles we face.

What that means personally for you and me is this: when we suffer, when our prayers go unanswered, and when our loved ones let us down, Someone has been there before us. It also means that while we may not get all of the answers we want, we do have a Friend who understands us completely.

Notes

Notes